A GUIDED JOURNAL EXPERIENCE

braving *the* brokenness

*Tell your story to unlock your healing
and live wholeheartedly*

Xulon Press
2301 Lucien Way #415
Maitland, FL 32751
407.339.4217
www.xulonpress.com

NICOLE EDGMOND

A GUIDED JOURNAL EXPERIENCE

braving *the*
brokenness

*Tell your story to unlock your healing
and live wholeheartedly*

XULON PRESS

To all the women who have gathered around my table,
sat in my living room,
or bravely walked through my office doors:
Thank you for the opportunity you provide for each of us
to hear the sound of Heaven and rewrite the stories of our lives.

Contents

How to Get Started

——∞∞∞——

You can do this guided journal alone. You can. But I believe it would be most beneficial to do it in a group. Most people are living in a story we know nothing about. Maybe you have stories you've yet to tell. Stories filled with shame, doubt, and painful emotions. We need each other. We need voices of hope and encouragement. We need to know we are not alone in our struggle. So, I highly recommend you gather a few friends and go through this journey together!

Group Size Due to the intimate nature of this group it is best to have 3 to 6 members. Always pray and ask God who you should invite. This group is for women (or men) who will commit to growing in God and authentic relationships with each other. Once you start your group, do not add new members. If you are a part of a larger group, then you can break into smaller groups to ensure everyone has time to share. Consider that each person will need 15-30 minutes to share their story.

Timing Typically, the group will last anywhere from 2-4 hours. This can be structured to meet your time constraints. If you choose to eat together before you start (which I highly recommend!) add 30-45 minutes for time to eat and connect, and then add 15-30 minutes per person for sharing. There will be times that the group lingers on a specific topic and other times when the story is quick and shared with ease.

Scheduling You can meet every week, every other week, or once a month. Keep in mind that this group is meant to help you foster intimacy and vulnerability. It takes time. It is an emotional process. Decide together what timeline best fits your group. How much time do your members need to prepare and come ready for the next story?

Hosting A safe, open, and comfortable space is always the best place to host this type of group. Someone's comfy home is preferable. Candles lit. Pillows and blankets available. A place where people feel invited and safe to cry, laugh, and be emotionally present.

Materials Every participant should have the *Braving the Brokenness* book and guided journal, which includes space for journaling and writing your story. If you would like more guidance or a brief introduction to each story, you can access videos on YouTube under Nicole Edgmond.

Getting Started/Facilitator Every group should appoint a facilitator. Please access the video for facilitators on my YouTube channel for more detailed suggestions and encouragement! ***In your first meeting*** introduce yourselves, share a few things about your life, and review the sections below. This time and information is vital for the health and success of your group! Read it aloud. Have discussions. Make sure everyone is on the same page and ready to begin. The facilitator will keep an eye on the clock during discussions. I know this can feel awkward at first. It is important to gauge where the Spirit is leading, but also important everyone has the opportunity to participate. After the initial FIRST meeting, follow the group outline below.

Structuring the 12 story sessions Sharing a meal together is a great way to connect before you jump into the heart of the matter! Below is a suggested schedule to follow:

- Gather to eat and connect. (30-45 minutes)
- Begin the story time with prayer. (1-2 minutes)
- Read the section <u>Walking in Truth</u> as a reminder before you share your stories. (3 minutes)
- Read the story prompt for that week. (3 minutes)
- Ask someone to share their story! Typically, it will take 5 minutes or less to read the prepared story. Then 10-20 minutes to walk your friend through the "listening" process. They do most of the talking. You listen then ask the questions. It would be helpful to have the section, <u>Learning to Ask Important Questions</u>, on page 10, available when you are ready to ask questions. Give each person time to feel heard and encouraged. (15-30 minutes per person)
- End the group by watching the YouTube video for the next story, or simply read aloud the story title in your journal, and close with prayer. (5-10 minutes)

Enjoy the journey!

Introduction

⬥

As a Christian Counselor I have the privilege of meeting with people as they bravely share their story. Many people feel disconnected, unknown, and alone in the quest to live their life well. Hiding behind a veil of spirituality, perfection, or service, they remain virtually unknown, emotionally disconnected, and purposeless.

And these are people in church.

"Church" often consists of a fifteen-minute break before a one-hour service begins. People dart in and out of church doors glibly asking, "How are you?" After a short pause, we typically add, "Good? Good!!" We smile real big and hug. Smiling on the outside, dying on the inside. We worship for three songs, pray for five minutes, listen to a message for 35 minutes, close the service with a song, and a quick "Be blessed. Go change your world for Jesus!" Maybe we share about a "bad day" quickly (and shamefully) adding, "But God is good!" And off we go, back to our homes, jobs, and relationships feeling even more alone.

Disconnection is not a church caused problem–it is a cultural problem. We live in a culture that values perfection, outward appearance, competence, and success. The church is not exempt from this influence. But what is a Christian to do when they feel less than perfect, incompetent, unhappy, or stuck? Who do they talk to? Where do they go with their pain and disappointment?

Are all the broken people that make up a church even qualified to hear each other's pain-filled stories without causing more damage, or rejection? Can the church listen and love people where they are at, in the middle of pain, shame, and heartache?

I believe we can. But we must create the space, a safe place, to come and tell our story. We must learn to listen well to the stories of others. We must listen in a way that ushers in healing and releases the power of God to enable others to see their true selves and walk in their God given destiny. This is no small feat, but this is essential to building a healthy, thriving church.

In building a brave and authentic community, I believe we can journey towards healing, redemption, and intimacy with God and others through sharing the hard stories of our lives. This journal is a guide to sharing your story in a healthy, safe environment that invites personal healing and redemption through Christ-like community. Anyone can lead this group! Every chapter in the book, *Braving the Brokenness*, coordinates with a themed story prompt for you, and your group, to write your story. The book gives more detailed information and teaching as it relates to each story. Use the tools below to lead your group and then start writing! I can't wait to hear how God moves in and through your brave hearts!

The Stories You'll Share

—⚬⚬⚬—

Bible studies are amazing and needed for spiritual growth. This is not a Bible study. There are scriptures mixed in and through this process, but the focus of this group is about learning how to live in vulnerability, courage, and grace as you share your story with fellow travelers. This group is about building a community that knows the real you, accepts you, and loves you. This group is about belonging and becoming.

While our lives hold countless stories, I believe these 12 stories will guide you and your friends into deeper freedom and wholeness as you lean in to listen and sit back to share. This process will encourage and benefit those who are walking closely with God, and those who are just beginning their God-journey. The story writing process is incredibly brave and sometimes a bit scary! Seek to encourage one another no matter where each of you "started". The best advice is to remember you are all learning and growing together! There are some things you just haven't learned yet, so walk in grace toward others and yourself.

You will write these 12 Stories.

1. God Speaks
2. When Shame Writes Your Story

1

Building a Brave Community

Your current story begs you to press into the chapters
of your life you've tried to dismiss,
and face your untold story with courage as you learn
the truth that will set you free.
This truth boldly paving the way for you
to become your truest self
and live your most fulfilling life.
As you look back on yesterday, you catch a vision
for tomorrow and ask yourself,
"What will my future chapters hold?"

The Battle For Your Soul

The real truth of braving the brokenness is that you are made for more. There is a battle for your soul. With each story you will be brought one step closer to naming, engaging, and defeating the very real enemy that seeks to kill your heart, soul, and destiny! Every story shared hold keys; opportunities to expose faulty lies and toxic thoughts, and equally divine opportunities to usher you and your friends into the truths and promises of God, releasing you into your God given destinies.

3

"The thief comes only to steal and kill and destroy,
I came that they may have life, and have it abundantly."
John 10:10 ESV

"For we are not fighting against flesh and blood enemies,
but against evil rulers and authorities of the unseen world,
against mighty powers in this dark world,
and against evil spirits in the heavenly places."
Ephesians 6:12 NLT

Let Truth Lead You

Before you begin, realize that every person is on a different path in their journey with God. Every step of your journey is significant. So instead of looking back to where you wished or hoped or thought you should have done this, or that, set your eyes ahead. Determine now–you will share your story only to move forward. The beauty of life in God is that you do not have to "do anything" to have authority to claim his truths. They are yours. Take hold of these truths and let the journey begin!

"But we have the mind of Christ."
1 Corinthians 2:16 NIV

"So, God created man in his own image,
in the image of God he created them,
male and female he created them."
Genesis 1:27 NIV

"Christ is in you."
Colossians 1:27 MSG

4

*"His divine power has given us everything
we need for living a godly life.
We have received all of this by coming to know him,
the one who called us to himself by means of his marvelous
glory and excellence. Through these he has given us
great and precious promises.
These are promises that enable you to share
his divine nature."*
2 Peter 1:3,4a NLT

*"May God give you the spirit of wisdom and revelation,
so that you may know him better.
I pray that the eyes of your heart may be enlightened
in order that you may know the hope
to which he has called you, the riches of his glorious
inheritance in his holy people."*
Ephesians 1:17b,18 NIV

God fills us to the fullest measure when we ask him for divine wisdom. You are the vessel. He is the Lover, Healer, and Hope Giver. You have been made in the very image of God and have the mind of Christ. This means you can think like Him, listen like Him, and love like Him. Christ is in you! This will be essential in understanding how to journey well with the people God puts in your life. Your ability to build a healthy community hinges on your dependence of the Holy Spirit and God's love being poured out through you.

Tracy's Story

Facing her diagnosis of anthrophobia (fear of humans), also known as social phobia, Tracy decided to join a Bible Study. After two years of learning God's word, solidifying her identity in Christ, and beginning to live free from fear, she jumped into a Brave Community group. Just two years prior to this, she had never spoken in a group setting, let alone shared personal details of her story. This is her testimony.

"There are chapters in your life that you just don't read out loud! These are the chapters filled with too much pain, shame, hurt, and things you wouldn't ever want to go through again. This group opened a space for us, a safe space where we knew it would be ok to go back to that place we never intended to visit again. We knew there would be no condemnation, only supportive voices.

Going through the physical act of writing down my experiences and taking the time to relive them, allowed me to revisit them with God and see how He had been working on my behalf in ways I never imagined. Speaking my story out loud was physically freeing and actually felt like a weight was lifted off of my life. Hearing feedback from others made me feel validated, supported, and most importantly, not alone.

I learned I am not so different from others. Also, what I say and think on a daily basis has much to do with what I have been through in my past. I began to see how essential it is to look back for the purpose of moving forward, knowing God's plan for my life. Bad things are going to happen but it is just a part of the story. It does not need to stay a stronghold. God's love has come in, loosened the past' grasp on me and healed me. It has created a space for his peace to settle into my life."

Get ready to embark on an amazing journey! Press into the Holy Spirit and open your heart to love well. This is the way to freedom for you and your friends! I am praying for you to encounter the truth that will set you free!

The Importance of Vision

"Where there is no vision, the people perish."
Proverbs 29:18 KJV

The *goals* of this GROUP are to:

- connect to God in a more meaningful and deeper way.
- recognize the false self and all its unhealthy ways of relating.
- create new rhythms and processes to handle hard emotions, pain, shame, and other triggers.
- come to a place of love and acceptance of the person God has created us to be.
- create community that connects us to one another through encouragement, strength, support, empathy, and understanding.
- be authentic in our struggles and make ourselves fully known.
- listen with the ears of Christ. To really hear the hurt, the joy, the suffering. To rejoice when they rejoice. To weep when they weep. Love sees, feels, and then acts.
- listen to the Holy Spirit as each person talks and to call forth the good that is there.

- ask questions to understand more genuinely their relationship with God, self, and others.
- keep the ultimate end goal always in our mind–that all other longings, desires, or hopes would take their place behind our first love. That we would long for God above all else.

"For if they fall, one will lift up his companion.
But woe to him who is alone when he falls,
For he has no one to help him up."
Ecclesiastes 4:10 NKJV

Learning to Become Listeners that Lead to Soul Care

<hr />

Learning to listen takes practice. Our natural inclination is to be self-centered. Without divine intervention, we are lousy at thinking of others above ourselves! True listening is other-centered. These three steps will be helpful as you learn new rhythms of listening. I am grateful for the work of Larry Crabb. These concepts have been gleaned from his expertise and his beautiful book, *Soul Talk, The Language God Longs for Us to Speak*. I highly recommend reading his book if you want to delve deeper into understanding the language of the soul.

1. **Listen.** Live curious. Linger with the story teller. Do not speak. Ears open. Eyes of your heart enlightened.
2. **Ask.** Seek to understand by way of asking questions. Stay with the story teller as they begin to have revelation. Do not share your thoughts. Only ask questions. Listen longer. Go deeper. Ask more questions.
3. **Speak.** Only when God nudges you to do so–speak words of affirmation or a scripture God puts on your heart. Speak to who they *really are*, not to their struggle, but to the redeemed person they are in Christ.

1) Learning to Listen with Holy Curiosity

Listening with holy curiosity requires you engage the speaker with your heart and soul. Enter into someone's story and ask yourself, what is the real battle they are facing? Tune in to the spirit and have a heart bent to the Lord. Listen beyond the story and hear the deeper struggle that rumbles through both the spoken and unspoken words. This is not easy, but remember you have the mind of Christ. You can ask Jesus to help you hear the inaudible battle cry. The real war. The deeper issues that hide behind a story. The issues of identity, worth and most certainly faulty views of self, God, and others. Many people have never shared their stories, let alone named the issues that are held captive by their silence. It will be your job to sit still long enough to listen, not with human ears, but with the ears of Christ. Wait. Listen more.

It is NOT your job to offer advice, try to change the person, or have all the answers. Relief is not your goal. Neither is recovery. You are not there to solve any problems. This is not about you. Try to stay away from the phrase, "I can relate."

Let the pain be present in the room. Let the tears come. Do not be too quick to escape the uncomfortable feelings that may arise. Pain needs space. Embrace the God given empathy that arises within you.

Not all stories hold pain by the way! Some need celebration and laughter and joy. Sometimes people need you to throw some confetti, dance, and eat cake. Life can be hard and when there is a victory, celebrate! Don't be too quick to focus on all the hard stuff of life. There is a time for everything. Don't skip celebrating!

As you listen, you will, at times, find yourself annoyed, frustrated, disengaged, angry, and a plethora of other non-Christ like responses to a human soul in conflict. This is not your true self. You are made in the image of God. Ask yourself, "What is getting in the way of me listening to the voice of God?" Confess your judgements, selfish tendencies, lack of empathy, and repent to Christ in that very moment (in your mind) and return to listening. The enemy of your friend's soul wants nothing more than for you to be distracted, judgmental, and disengaged.

2) Learning to Ask Important Questions

After you have listened, waited, and stayed present to the story your friend has shared, you will begin the process of asking questions. The goal in this step is to invite the storyteller to go deeper. What is God up to in their story? What is the real battle? In order for you to have any power to speak into their story (which is the last step) you must allow the Holy Spirit to bring light and revelation to you and your friend.

Some questions to ask:

1. Can you tell me more?
2. Do you feel "good enough" in this story? Why or why not?
3. What is the story you are telling yourself now?
4. What were you really wanting in that situation?
5. What are you longing for today?
6. Did it feel like God's goodness?
7. What do you believe about God in the middle of this struggle?
8. What are you afraid of?
9. How are you connecting to God through this?
10. What is the truth?

11. How is Satan tempting you? What is he saying to you?
12. Have you felt this way before? When?
13. What is God showing you through all of this?
14. Can you hear God speaking to you?
15. What do you want?
16. What have you come to believe about yourself?

As you continue to ask questions, you are listening with the ears of Christ. In asking these questions you will begin to see the battle in their soul to fully trust God. These questions will help you uncover the plan of the enemy and hear the heartbeat of God in the story they are sharing. You ask questions to understand more where they have been and how that story has shaped their thinking, feeling, and choosing. Remember, you are not trying to fix anyone, solve the problems they are facing, give advice, or offer solutions. You are listening with these two questions in mind:

Where do I hear the voice of the enemy in this story? What is he saying?

Where do I hear the voice of God in this story? What is the Spirit saying?

3) Learning to Speak the Words of God

Once you have engaged the heart of the battle and leaned in to hear the heartbeat of Heaven for your friend, you are ready to speak. Do not rush talking. If it comes from **you,** it is empty talk. If it is **Spirit** breathed, it will bring life. Slow down and realize that your ability to pour into your friend depends on what you have been filled up with. The truth is, you cannot give what you do not possess. So, this is your wake-up call to press into God daily. When you know God's truths, you can speak God's truths to others.

1. Tell them who they are, as it aligns with Biblical truth.
2. Share a specific scripture.
3. Tell them how it made you feel to experience their vulnerability–their true self. This is about experiencing them as they really are–honest, trusting, open, and willing.

The goal of gathering together to listen to the stories is to draw our friends into the deepest longing of their soul. We want them to know and believe God as the only ONE who can meet every need, fill every longing, and provide their deepest satisfaction. We want our friends to *want God more* than they want anything else: more than safety, better relationships, pain free living, security in money, answers to hard questions, and even comfort.

God's words are life giving. They will bring hope and truth, replacing despair and lies. His heart beats for freedom and healing. His desire will always be to draw the storyteller into a great romance. Our testimonies unlocking the hope of His whisper of love in a broken world. Do you have the words of God on your mouth and in your heart? This is your beautiful opportunity to take inventory and ask yourself some hard questions. God will use you no matter where you are at in the journey. He only asks if you are ready to listen. If so, get close to God. Hear His whispers and then speak.

> *"And the Lord will guide you continually*
> *and satisfy your desire in scorched places*
> *and make your bones strong, and you shall be*
> *like a watered garden, whose waters do not fail."*
> Isaiah 58:11 ESV

Walking in Truth

"Sanctify them in the truth; your word is truth."
John 17:17 ESV

Some ***key truths*** Brave Community Groups are built upon.

Read these together and then post this list somewhere where you will read it out loud daily.

1. **I am loved.** Simply because you are alive. When you do the right thing and the wrong thing, you are STILL loved. You are loved because God died for you, gave up his life for you, and calls you HIS beloved son or daughter. (John 3:16, Romans 5:8, Romans 8:1, 35-39)

2. **I am chosen.** Simply because you said yes to God, you belong. You are in a family and you are wanted. This is not built on the merit of gifts, but on your inheritance as God's child. (Ephesians 1:4, John 15:16)

3. **I am worthy.** Simply because you are breathing you have value, worth, and acceptance in your being. You are not more or less worthy because of what you do or what you have not done, what you struggle with, or what you succeed in. Your worth is never based on performance. (Isaiah 43, Psalm 139:13-18)

4. **I am needed.** Your beauty and unique personality are needed in this world. Your voice is needed. (Ephesians 2:10, 1 John 4:12)

5. **I am imperfect.** Sometimes you are a bit untidy, broken, and tender. Working through your weaknesses is called "process" and we all have to walk in it. You don't have to have it all together. It's ok to be honest. Don't buy into the lie you have to "clean up" to come in. (2 Corinthians 12:9)

6. **I am worth celebrating.** Together we gather as a reminder that no matter where we are at in the journey we can celebrate! Every time we gather, we remember to bless, encourage, and celebrate those we are so privileged to know on a deeper level. We always start here: Laugh, share, celebrate. (Ecclesiastes 8:15)

7. **I choose whose story wins.** Every event holds the opportunity for the sound of Hell to rule you (The voice of Satan) or the sound of Heaven to lead you (The voice of Jesus) and your story will say as much. Be prepared to discern between the sound of Heaven and the sound of Hell. Be prepared to choose between life and death. (Deuteronomy 30:15-20, 1 Peter 5:8, Jeremiah 29:11)

8. **I am safe.** When you believe the things listed above, you can dare to be vulnerable. When you hold to the commitment to see others in this very same light that you long to be seen in, you create a safe place for everyone. We are called to be safe for others and we can only do that when we see each other as God sees us. We are to bear the image of Christ. (2 Corinthians 3:18)

Brave Group
Participation Agreement

⎯⎯⎯⎯⎯⎯⎯⎯

1. ___I will meditate on the truths___ above until I believe them in my own life.
2. ___I will tell the truth___. I will be vulnerable and risk looking foolish for the sake of growth and freedom, becoming more the woman God created me to be.
3. ___I will listen with curiosity___ and ask myself, "___What's the real battle___ my friend is facing?"
4. ___I will press into the Spirit___ as He leads me to see what could be in this friend of mine.
5. ___I will face the mess that comes up in me___ as my friend shares, ___confess my sin___, ___and remove all judgment.___
6. ___I will think "Theme"___ as my friend is sharing, knowing there is always a hidden story and shaping events to be explored. The initial story leads to more stories and more understanding of the two stories that are at odds. Only then will I begin to ask questions.
7. ___I will embrace the goal that the most important thing in this whole process is the desire to see my friend long for Jesus more___ than a good life, quick fix, pain free life or anything else. ___I will fight the urge to run, fix things, or shut down.___ I will remember I am the conduit between

my friend and Jesus. I will listen. I will wait. Only then will I speak His voice.

8. ___I will cultivate trust by keeping all stories and experiences confidential.___
9. ___I will come prepared with my story___.
10. ___I will be prayed up___ and ready to lead with my ears, not my mouth.

I am committed to abiding by these guidelines as a participant in this Brave Community Group.

Name_____ Date_____

Rewrite the value of these guidelines in your own words below.

Preparing to Write Your Story

—∞∞—

Some helpful suggestions before you jump into writing your story:

1. Always start with prayer. Invite God into your thinking. Take some time to get alone with God and work through the journal questions in the ***Think About It*** section. These questions are meant to stir your heart as it relates to the topic. Sit with God. Ask Him to reveal the story He wants you to share. Don't write the story just yet.

2. After a few days of thinking and praying about the topic– choose a story. Then sit in a quiet place and ***Write Your Story.*** Do not edit the story. Just write. This is not a contest. You do not need perfect grammar or eloquent poetic speech. This is the raw you. Just get the story out.

3. Wait a day or two and reread your story. Is there anything you need to add or change? If not, then let that be your final story to share.

4. Once you have shared your story and your friends have asked questions and spoken truth where it was needed, write what your friends tell you in the ***Listen for the Sound of Heaven*** section. Sometimes you will learn new things, hear new perspectives, and receive fresh revelation. It is important to remember that all truth given to you must line up with God's Word. While there are times for correction in the body of

Christ, this is the time to speak words of truth, encouragement, and hope.

5. Now you can write the NEW story. You will do this on your
   own, not to share, but for your personal growth and becoming.
   The **_Rewrite The Story_** section is where you rewrite the
   story of your past with the truths of God interwoven and
   embraced. Where the lies of the enemy once screamed loud,
   you rewrite your story (if necessary) based on the truths that
   were revealed.

Let's get started!

Braving the Brokenness:
Write Your Story

———⋘⋙———

Story 1

God Speaks

Writing a new story requires that you actually believe God will speak to you in a new way, a way you may never have heard before. His voice is powerful. His voice is real. He spoke and there was light. You were made by the voice of God. (Genesis 1:3)

And God said, "Let us make human beings in our image, to be
like us. So God created human beings in his own image."
Genesis 1:26a, 27a NLT

In the Old Testament God spoke to Moses (Exodus 20:22), Abraham (Genesis 22:11) and through his prophets (Daniel 4:31) and now we have full access to hearing God through his Son!

"Long ago, at many times and in many ways,
God spoke to our forefathers by the prophets,
but in these last days he has spoken to us by his Son."
Hebrews 1:1,2 NIV

Today we have a Good Shepherd, Jesus, who leads us by still waters. His voice is kind, loving, and gentle.

"My sheep hear my voice, and I know them,
and they follow me."
John 10:27 ESV

Believing that God *still* speaks is essential in this journey. God speaking to you is the very thing that will change your life. But you cannot hear God if you do not <u>ask God</u> to speak to you. Much of this journey is about believing that God will speak intimately to you and give you words of life and hope to speak over yourself and others. When you ask God, you wait. You wait for his voice. You wait for the sound of Heaven to fill your mind, heart, and soul. His voice brings peace.

"Call to me and I will answer you and will tell you great and hidden things that you have not known."
Jeremiah 33:3 ESV

Here are three ways I have experienced God speaking to me:

1. God speaks to me through the Bible. The Bible is the most trusted form of communication with our Father. (Hebrews 4:12, 2 Timothy 3:16)
2. God speaks to me in whispers. Whispers form in my mind and I know it was not a thought that I would naturally think. It is the voice of God directly spoken to my heart. He is quiet. So I get quiet. I get alone in nature or a special spot. He is intimate. His words bring life. (1 Kings 19:12)
3. God speaks to me through other people. God will use pastors, mentors, friends, and other people to affirm his truths. Sometimes it is through a song, a book, a sermon, etc. But God places me in the right place, at the right time, to hear his heart through these other people. (Hebrews 12:1)

Think About It

Where are you in your journey of hearing the voice of God? Do you believe God speaks to you personally? How?

_____

_____

_____

_____

_____

_____

_____

_____

_____

_____

_____

_____

_____

_____

_____

_____

_____

_____

_____

_____

_____

_____

_____

_____

_____

_____

_____

_____

_____

Have you asked God to speak personal words of encouragement, hope, and love to you? What did you hear?

_____

_____

_____

_____

_____

_____

_____

_____

_____

_____

_____

_____

_____

_____

_____

_____

_____

_____

_____

_____

_____

_____

_____

_____

_____

_____

_____

_____

_____

_____

Have you asked God to use you to speak an encouraging word to a friend? What happened?

_____

_____

_____

_____

_____

_____

_____

_____

_____

_____

_____

_____

_____

_____

_____

_____

_____

_____

_____

_____

_____

_____

_____

_____

_____

_____

_____

_____

_____

If you don't have a story yet or this is new to you, then write about your desire to hear God speak.

_____
_____
_____
_____
_____
_____
_____
_____
_____
_____
_____
_____
_____
_____
_____
_____
_____
_____
_____
_____
_____
_____
_____
_____
_____
_____
_____

Write Your Story

Now, write a story about _When God Speaks_ to share with your group:

_____

_____

_____

_____

_____

_____

_____

_____

_____

_____

_____

_____

_____

_____

_____

_____

_____

_____

_____

_____

_____

_____

_____

_____

_____

_____

_____

_____

_____
_____
_____
_____
_____
_____
_____
_____
_____
_____
_____
_____
_____
_____
_____
_____
_____
_____
_____
_____
_____
_____
_____
_____
_____
_____
_____
_____

Listen for the Sound of Heaven

After you have shared your story write what the Lord spoke to you through your friends. What did He say? What is stirring in your heart?

_____

_____

_____

_____

_____

_____

_____

_____

_____

_____

_____

_____

_____

_____

_____

_____

_____

_____

_____

_____

_____

_____

_____

_____

_____

_____

Rewrite the Story

Do you need to do any REWRITING in your story? If so, write about the lie you were believing regarding hearing from God and rewrite the story in truth.

_____

_____

_____

_____

_____

_____

_____

_____

_____

_____

_____

_____

_____

_____

_____

_____

_____

_____

_____

_____

_____

_____

_____

_____

_____

_____

_____

Story 2

When Shame Writes Your Story

Shame says I am unworthy. I am not enough.

We all long to be loved, accepted, and valued. We all long to be connected and feel a sense of belonging. We all long for a purpose that is bigger than ourselves. And yet, somehow, somewhere along the way, we were told that we were not enough. Not smart enough, pretty enough, good enough, interesting enough, worthy enough–for that job, that person, that love. And we believe these voices. We believe the messages that they sent. Their words leaving us tossed to and fro in a sea of shame.

The voice of shame speaks often and loudly. Our bodies feel it. We get hot and sweaty. Our hearts start to beat fast and the desire to disappear into the floor is strong!

But did you know that before you could make choices–good or bad, obey or disobey, work hard or be lazy, get amazing grades or flunk each class–you were created wonderful *before* you could decide you were not. This is still the truth. No matter what.

> *"For you created my inmost being, you knit me together in my mother's womb. I praise you because I am fearfully and wonderfully made; your works are wonderful, I know that full well."*
> Psalm 139:13-14 NIV

No matter what you have DONE, SAID, BELIEVED, or EXPERIENCED–you are *enough*.

You must know where shame is operating and how it is impacting you. Shame loses its power when it is revealed. So, name your shame–the lie of the enemy–those words and messages that haunt you.

Name the place that shame first spoke to your soul.

Think About It

What voices of shame do you most often hear in your mind? What are the negative thoughts you think about yourself?

_____

_____

_____

_____

_____

_____

_____

_____

_____

_____

_____

_____

_____

_____

_____

_____

_____

_____

_____

_____

_____

_____

_____

_____

_____

_____

_____

_____

When was the FIRST TIME you remember thinking a shameful thought about yourself? What happened? Where were you?

_____

_____

_____

_____

_____

_____

_____

_____

_____

_____

_____

_____

_____

_____

_____

_____

_____

_____

_____

_____

_____

_____

_____

_____

_____

_____

Are there any lies you have believed in your life that have caused shame to feel like truth?

_____

_____

_____

_____

_____

_____

_____

_____

_____

_____

_____

_____

_____

_____

_____

_____

_____

_____

_____

_____

_____

_____

_____

_____

_____

_____

_____

_____

_____

Write Your Story

Now, write your story, _When Shame Writes My Story,_ and share it with your group:

_____

_____

_____

_____

_____

_____

_____

_____

_____

_____

_____

_____

_____

_____

_____

_____

_____

_____

_____

_____

_____

_____

_____

_____

_____

_____

_____

_____

_____

_____

_____

_____

_____

_____

_____

_____

_____

_____

_____

_____

_____

_____

_____

_____

_____

_____

_____

_____

_____

_____

_____

_____

_____

_____

_____

_____

_____

_____

_____

_____

_____

_____

_____

_____

_____

_____

_____

_____

_____

_____

_____

_____

_____

_____

_____

_____

_____

_____

_____

_____

_____

_____

_____

_____

_____

_____

_____

_____

Listen for the Sound of Heaven

After you have shared your story in your group write what the Lord spoke to you through your friends. What did He say? What is stirring in your heart?

_____

_____

_____

_____

_____

_____

_____

_____

_____

_____

_____

_____

_____

_____

_____

_____

_____

_____

_____

_____

_____

_____

_____

_____

_____

_____

_____

_____

_____

_____

_____

_____

_____

_____

_____

_____

_____

_____

_____

_____

_____

_____

_____

_____

_____

_____

_____

_____

_____

_____

_____

_____

_____

_____

_____

Rewrite the Story

Do you need to do any REWRITING in your story? If so, write about the lie you were believing regarding shame and rewrite the story in truth.

_____

_____

_____

_____

_____

_____

_____

_____

_____

_____

_____

_____

_____

_____

_____

_____

_____

_____

_____

_____

_____

_____

_____

_____

_____

_____

_____

_____

_____

_____

_____

_____

_____

_____

_____

_____

_____

_____

_____

_____

_____

_____

_____

_____

_____

_____

_____

_____

_____

_____

_____

_____

_____

_____

_____

Story 3

Pain and Loss

"Not one thing in your life is more important than figuring out how to live in the face of unspoken pain."
Ann Voskamp, *The Broken Way*

Tragedy and pain are a part of life. It is an inevitable reality. You will have troubles. You will face obstacles. You will suffer. There will be loss. But there is hope and God promises to take tragedy and turn it into something used for good.

"In this world you will have trouble, but take heart!
I have overcome the world."
John 16:33 NIV

Has time and space and healing come to you since the tragedy, the loss, the pain? Maybe you are breathing, but you are not really living. Tragedy can do that to a soul. It can suck the life out of you, but still give you just enough air to breathe. Take a deep breath now. God wants to hear about your pain.

Think About It

Where are you in your journey through your tragedy or loss? What are your greatest losses? What happened?

_____

_____

_____

_____

_____

_____

_____

_____

_____

_____

_____

_____

_____

_____

_____

_____

_____

_____

_____

_____

_____

_____

_____

_____

_____

_____

_____

_____

_____

Is there a pain so deep you never thought you would see your-self through it? Are you through it?

_____

_____

_____

_____

_____

_____

_____

_____

_____

_____

_____

_____

_____

_____

_____

_____

_____

_____

_____

_____

_____

_____

_____

_____

_____

_____

_____

_____

_____

_____

Has God redeemed the pain? How?

_____

_____

_____

_____

_____

_____

_____

_____

_____

_____

_____

_____

_____

_____

_____

_____

_____

_____

_____

_____

_____

_____

_____

_____

_____

_____

_____

_____

_____

_____

_____

_____

If not, where or how do you feel stuck in the pain of your story?

_____

_____

_____

_____

_____

_____

_____

_____

_____

_____

_____

_____

_____

_____

_____

_____

_____

_____

_____

_____

_____

_____

_____

_____

_____

_____

_____

_____

_____

_____

Write Your Story

Now, write your story on _Pain and Loss_ that you will share with your group:

_____

_____

_____

_____

_____

_____

_____

_____

_____

_____

_____

_____

_____

_____

_____

_____

_____

_____

_____

_____

_____

_____

_____

_____

_____

_____

_____

_____

_____

_____

_____

Listen for the Sound of Heaven

After you have shared your story in your group write what the Lord spoke to you through your friends. What did He say? What is stirring in your heart?

_____

_____

_____

_____

_____

_____

_____

_____

_____

_____

_____

_____

_____

_____

_____

_____

_____

_____

_____

_____

_____

_____

_____

_____

_____

_____

_____

_____

_____

_____

Rewrite the Story

Do you need to do any REWRITING in your story? If so, write about the lie you were believing regarding your pain and rewrite the story in truth.

_____

_____

_____

_____

_____

_____

_____

_____

_____

_____

_____

_____

_____

_____

_____

_____

_____

_____

_____

_____

_____

_____

_____

_____

_____

_____

_____

Story 4

The Questions

When we experience pain it births questions in our soul. Often, we take the questions to our family, friends, the man or the woman, and ask them:

Do you see me?

Do you care about my pain?

Am I enough?

Do you think I am beautiful?

Do you delight in me?

Are you proud of me?

Am I loved? Just as I am?

Do I matter?

Will you fight for me?

You will struggle to find your place, your peace, your hope until these questions have been answered. But maybe you didn't know you could ask God these questions. Maybe you didn't know that God actually wanted you to be honest and raw and real with Him. Well, now you know. Now you can ask. Begin the vast and wonderful adventure of taking your questions to God.

Think About It

What questions linger in your soul?

_____

_____

_____

_____

_____

_____

_____

_____

_____

_____

_____

_____

_____

_____

_____

_____

_____

_____

_____

_____

_____

_____

_____

_____

_____

_____

_____

_____

_____

Where have you gone in the past to get your questions answered? What other voices have you turned to? What other ways have you sought out answers?

_____

_____

_____

_____

_____

_____

_____

_____

_____

_____

_____

_____

_____

_____

_____

_____

_____

_____

_____

_____

_____

_____

_____

_____

_____

_____

_____

_____

Did you know you could ask God these questions?

_____

_____

_____

_____

_____

_____

_____

_____

_____

_____

_____

_____

_____

_____

_____

_____

_____

_____

_____

_____

_____

_____

_____

_____

_____

_____

_____

_____

_____

_____

_____

Have you experienced God answering a question of your soul? What happened?

_____
_____
_____
_____
_____
_____
_____
_____
_____
_____
_____
_____
_____
_____
_____
_____
_____
_____
_____
_____
_____
_____
_____
_____
_____
_____
_____
_____
_____

Write Your Story

Now, write your story on _The Questions_ that you will share with your group:

_____

_____

_____

_____

_____

_____

_____

_____

_____

_____

_____

_____

_____

_____

_____

_____

_____

_____

_____

_____

_____

_____

_____

_____

_____

_____

_____

_____

_____

Listen for the Sound of Heaven

After you have shared your story in your group write what the Lord spoke to you through your friends. What did He say? What is stirring in your heart?

_____

_____

_____

_____

_____

_____

_____

_____

_____

_____

_____

_____

_____

_____

_____

_____

_____

_____

_____

_____

_____

_____

Rewrite the Story

Do you need to do any REWRITING in your story? If so, write about the lie you were believing regarding your questions and rewrite the story in truth.

_____

_____

_____

_____

_____

_____

_____

_____

_____

_____

_____

_____

_____

_____

_____

_____

_____

_____

_____

_____

_____

_____

_____

_____

_____

_____

_____

_____

_____

_____

_____

_____

_____

_____

_____

_____

_____

_____

_____

_____

_____

_____

_____

_____

_____

_____

_____

_____

_____

_____

_____

_____

_____

_____

_____

_____

_____

_____

_____
_____
_____
_____
_____
_____
_____
_____
_____
_____
_____
_____
_____
_____
_____
_____
_____
_____
_____
_____
_____
_____
_____
_____
_____
_____
_____
_____
_____
_____

Story 5

Trusting God

"To trust God in the light is nothing,
but trust him in the dark, that is faith."
Quote by
Charles H. Spurgeon

Trust. A confident expectation that packs a lot of weight. Everything hinges on trust.

Whom do you trust? Why do you trust them?

Trust is risk. Trust is scary. Trust is also essential to a life of freedom and joy.

But did you know that God does not actually ask you to trust people? He asks you to trust Him.

To really trust God, you need to know God. Completely. Fully. You need to know He is for you and not against you. You need to know He is faithful, good, kind, and all together lovely. He will never leave you or forsake you. He loves you, just as you are. He will come through. He will fight for you and wait for you and be with you.

There are truths you come to know and believe about God only by experiencing them. Life is NOT in your control. God asks you to trust Him with it all. Everything. Your heart. Your life. Your hurt. Your dreams. Everything.

He wants to show up for you, right in the middle of the mess. Did you know that?

"But I trust in your unfailing love; my heart rejoices in your salvation."
Psalm 13:5 NIV

Think About It

How has the journey to trust God been going for you?

_____

_____

_____

_____

_____

_____

_____

_____

_____

_____

_____

_____

_____

_____

_____

_____

_____

_____

_____

_____

_____

_____

_____

_____

_____

_____

_____

_____

_____

_____

What are the character traits of God that you have to come to fully believe in?

_____

_____

_____

_____

_____

_____

_____

_____

_____

_____

_____

_____

_____

_____

_____

_____

_____

_____

_____

_____

_____

_____

_____

_____

_____

_____

_____

_____

_____

_____

_____

_____

What experience led you to KNOW that God was worthy of your full, sold-out, surrendered trust?

_____

_____

_____

_____

_____

_____

_____

_____

_____

_____

_____

_____

_____

_____

_____

_____

_____

_____

_____

_____

_____

_____

_____

_____

_____

_____

_____

_____

_____

_____

_____

If you are not there yet, write about the struggle to trust God. What are the traits about God you doubt? What are the traits you long to experience for yourself?

_____

_____

_____

_____

_____

_____

_____

_____

_____

_____

_____

_____

_____

_____

_____

_____

_____

_____

_____

_____

_____

_____

_____

_____

_____

_____

_____

_____

_____

_____

_____

Write Your Story

Now, write your story on *Trusting God* that you will share with your group:

_____

_____

_____

_____

_____

_____

_____

_____

_____

_____

_____

_____

_____

_____

_____

_____

_____

_____

_____

_____

_____

_____

_____

_____

_____

_____

_____

_____

_____

_____

_____

_____

_____

_____

_____

_____

_____

_____

_____

_____

_____

_____

_____

_____

_____

_____

_____

_____

_____

_____

_____

_____

_____

_____

_____

_____

_____

_____

_____

_____

_____

_____

Listen for the Sound of Heaven

After you have shared your story in your group write what the Lord spoke to you through your friends. What did He say? What is stirring in your heart?

_____

_____

_____

_____

_____

_____

_____

_____

_____

_____

_____

_____

_____

_____

_____

_____

_____

_____

_____

_____

_____

_____

_____

_____

_____

Rewrite the Story

Do you need to do any REWRITING in your story? If so, write about the lie you were believing about the character of God and rewrite the story in truth.

_____

_____

_____

_____

_____

_____

_____

_____

_____

_____

_____

_____

_____

_____

_____

_____

_____

_____

_____

_____

_____

_____

_____

_____

_____

_____

_____

Story 6

Wired for Love

"You were made to be seen and known and loved deeply.
And it's ok to want what you were made for."
Angela Thomas, *Do You Think I'm Beautiful?*

You are wired for love. Deep within you is a place that hungers for a love that will complete you. This love will not be fulfilled by a man, a friend, or any other person. This love is meant to be found in the arms of God.

This longing for love creates a sense of restless wandering. You search for it. You wait for it. You were made for it. And this love, which comes from God, is meant to be experienced. It is meant to be felt. Not just in words, but with an encounter that changes you.

"You can only trust God as much as you know
you are loved by God."
Brennan Manning, *Ruthless Trust*

Having an encounter with God where he communicates his love to your soul is essential in your journey to trust God. If you do not know that God really loves you, sees you, and desires you then it will be very hard to believe anything else the Bible tells you. Imagine being willing to die, give away all your earthly possessions, and live unafraid of sickness, poverty, or death. I am not sure you can, *unless* you trust that no matter what–God loves you. You are His. ***You are His Beloved.***

Sometimes God uses people to accept you as you are, giving you a divine taste of the love of our good Father. God is always looking for ways to show you that you are loved. Sometimes, you miss it. Sometimes, you need to open your eyes and listen with your soul to hear the sound of Heaven.

> *"May you experience the love of Christ,*
> *though it is too great to understand fully.*
> *Then you will be made complete with all the fullness*
> *of life and power that comes from God."*
> Ephesians 3:19 NLT

Until you know that all the other loves will NEVER fully satisfy, you will keep chasing after them. But once you have tasted the love of God, you will hunger and thirst for his love like a parched runner on a hot summer day. His love satisfies, quenches, and fills. His love is a love worth chasing after. His love is a place of rest and belonging. His love truly is all you need.

> *"Those who seek the Lord lack no good thing."*
> Psalm 34:10b NIV

Think About It

When have you felt loved?

_____

_____

_____

_____

_____

_____

_____

_____

_____

_____

_____

_____

_____

_____

_____

_____

_____

_____

_____

_____

_____

_____

_____

_____

_____

_____

_____

_____

_____

_____

_____

_____

Did you believe it was God behind the "love" or did you credit a person?

_____

_____

_____

_____

_____

_____

_____

_____

_____

_____

_____

_____

_____

_____

_____

_____

_____

_____

_____

_____

_____

_____

_____

_____

_____

_____

_____

_____

_____

_____

Have you encountered the love of God in a specific, tangible way where you knew it was God?

What happened the day God told you, by way of another person, event, whisper, or glimpse of Him in nature, that HE LOVES YOU?

_____

_____

_____

_____

_____

_____

_____

_____

_____

_____

_____

_____

_____

_____

_____

_____

_____

_____

_____

_____

_____

_____

_____

_____

_____

_____

_____

_____

_____

_____

_____

Do you need to ask God to show you that He loves you? Go ahead and ask. Write about it here when He answers you!

_____

_____

_____

_____

_____

_____

_____

_____

_____

_____

_____

_____

_____

_____

_____

_____

_____

_____

_____

_____

_____

_____

_____

_____

_____

_____

Write Your Story

Now, write your story on _Wired for Love_ that you will share with your group:

_____

_____

_____

_____

_____

_____

_____

_____

_____

_____

_____

_____

_____

_____

_____

_____

_____

_____

_____

_____

_____

_____

_____

_____

_____

_____

_____

_____

_____

Listen for the Sound of Heaven

After you have shared your story in your group write what the Lord spoke to you through your friends. What did He say? What is stirring in your heart?

_____

_____

_____

_____

_____

_____

_____

_____

_____

_____

_____

_____

_____

_____

_____

_____

_____

_____

_____

_____

_____

_____

_____

_____

_____

_____

Rewrite the Story

Do you need to do any REWRITING in your story? If so, write about the lie you were believing about your worthiness to be loved and rewrite the story in truth.

_____

_____

_____

_____

_____

_____

_____

_____

_____

_____

_____

_____

_____

_____

_____

_____

_____

_____

_____

_____

_____

_____

_____

_____

_____

Story 7

Pain Relief

"Nothing teaches us about the preciousness of the Creator as much as when we learn the emptiness of everything else."
Charles Spurgeon, *Morning and Evening*

Pain is a part of life. We all want to feel better when we are hurting. It is tempting to avoid, numb, or run from pain at some point. Pain is not the problem. The things we turn to, our responses to pain, those are the messy parts of pain.

There are so many ways to avoid emotional and physical pain. You can eat more food, buy more clothes and cute shoes, redecorate your house or deep clean your house, gossip with a friend, veg out to tv shows, social media, movies, or novels. You can drink a glass of wine or two or three. Go on another vacation, seek out friends, family, sex. The ways to numb pain are as endless as the stars. There are so many ways you can seek to escape the quiet desperation of the soul.

While not everything listed above is wrong, when you turn to anything other than God for relief in the midst of hard feelings, then you are taking that blessing and turning it into an idol. And God is jealous for you. He will not relent until He has your full heart.

God calls you to come to Him for living water. To taste and see that He alone is life. He is the security, the passion, the longing, the love that you seek. Everyone is made to find their home in the love of Christ. This is the truth. He created you with needs and He wants to meet those needs. He is the *only one* who can meet those needs.

"My people have committed two sins, they have forsaken me,
the spring of living water, and have dug their own cisterns,
broken cisterns that cannot hold water."
Jeremiah 2:13 NIV

Pain will be used by a good God to let you know–*you need Him.*
When you turn to your broken cisterns (cracked pots)–those false
loves, plastic gods, and cheap imitations for life giving water–
they will only satisfy you for you a moment. Those faulty gods
will only create an emptiness deeper than the day before.

Jesus wants your heart. All of it. Every broken, bruised, battered,
and beat up place. Will you go to Him now? Will you choose
repentance? Will you choose to turn from your broken cisterns
that never really satisfy and drink deep from His living water?

"For He satisfies the thirsty and fills the hungry
with good things."
Psalm 107:9 NIV

Think About It

What are the broken cisterns in your life that have yet to quench your need for love and belonging?

_____

_____

_____

_____

_____

_____

_____

_____

_____

_____

_____

_____

_____

_____

_____

_____

_____

_____

_____

_____

_____

_____

_____

_____

_____

_____

_____

_____

Who are the people?

_____

_____

_____

_____

_____

_____

_____

_____

_____

_____

_____

_____

_____

_____

_____

_____

_____

_____

_____

_____

_____

_____

_____

_____

_____

_____

_____

_____

_____

_____

What are the places?

_____

_____

_____

_____

_____

_____

_____

_____

_____

_____

_____

_____

_____

_____

_____

_____

_____

_____

_____

_____

_____

_____

_____

_____

_____

_____

_____

_____

_____

_____

_____

_____

_____

What are the things?

_____

_____

_____

_____

_____

_____

_____

_____

_____

_____

_____

_____

_____

_____

_____

_____

_____

_____

_____

_____

_____

_____

_____

_____

_____

_____

_____

_____

_____

_____

_____

_____

Are you willing to give up these "go to sins" when you are in pain? Are you willing to go to God?

_____

_____

_____

_____

_____

_____

_____

_____

_____

_____

_____

_____

_____

_____

_____

_____

_____

_____

_____

_____

_____

_____

_____

_____

_____

_____

_____

_____

_____

_____

Write Your Story

Now, write your story on _Pain Relief_ that you will share with your group:

_____

_____

_____

_____

_____

_____

_____

_____

_____

_____

_____

_____

_____

_____

_____

_____

_____

_____

_____

_____

_____

_____

_____

_____

_____

_____

_____

_____

_____

_____

Listen for the Sound of Heaven

After you have shared your story in your group write what the Lord spoke to you through your friends. What did He say? What is stirring in your heart?

_____

_____

_____

_____

_____

_____

_____

_____

_____

_____

_____

_____

_____

_____

_____

_____

_____

_____

_____

_____

_____

_____

_____

_____

_____

_____

_____

_____

_____

_____

_____

_____

_____

_____

_____

_____

_____

_____

_____

_____

_____

_____

_____

_____

_____

_____

_____

_____

_____

_____

_____

_____

_____

_____

_____

_____

_____

_____

_____

_____

_____

_____

_____

Rewrite the Story

Do you need to do any REWRITING in your story? If so, write about the lie you were believing about relief and satisfaction and rewrite the story in truth.

_____

_____

_____

_____

_____

_____

_____

_____

_____

_____

_____

_____

_____

_____

_____

_____

_____

_____

_____

_____

_____

_____

_____

_____

_____

Story 8

Forgiveness

We must develop and maintain the capacity to forgive.
He who is devoid of the power to forgive
is devoid of the power to love.
There is some good in the worst of us and
some evil in the best of us.
When we discover this, we are less prone
to hate our enemies.
Quote by Martin Luther King, Jr.

Some people feel pretty comfortable with unforgiveness. They have their reasons. Mostly, people do not want to forgive because the offense created intense pain: emotional, mental, relational, physical, and spiritual. They have the scars to prove it. And sometimes forgiveness seems like saying to the offender, *It's no big deal. You are off the hook now. It didn't matter.*

This creates a sense of panic. One might think, *"Who will validate my pain if I forgive? If I forgive am I saying that my pain is not real, not significant? What do I do with my pain if I forgive?"*

God has a clear way to handle the sin of other people. It is a command actually. He calls us to forgive. When we trust God, we obey God. We know His commands are for our good.

"If you forgive others their trespasses, your heavenly Father
will also forgive you, but if you do not forgive others their
trespasses, neither will your Father forgive your trespasses."
Matthew 6:14 ESV

Forgiveness is often misunderstood. Here are some key truths.

1. Forgiveness is for me, not the offender.
2. Forgiveness frees me from the power of the one who hurt or offended me.
3. To forgive does not mean to forget, ignore, or deny the offense.
4. Forgiveness does not equal restoration.
5. Forgiveness does not equal trust.
6. Forgiveness is not an option; it is a command from God.
7. Forgiveness places God as Judge. He will exact vengeance.
8. Everyone is in need of forgiveness, including me.

Think about your life and your sin. Where are you weak? Broken? Flawed? Think about the grace given to you. Sometimes the person you need to forgive is yourself. See yourself held in the hands of God. You are forgiven, safe, and completely loved.

Now, God asks you to let go of the one who hurt you. Keep the truths in mind. All you are doing here is saying, *"God, I see my need to forgive and I will let go of the one who offended me. I trust you to lead them, work in them, and ultimately heal them. I trust you to be judge and juror over their life."* See yourself placing your offender in the hands of God. Leave them in God's hands. Let go. Walk away.

Forgiveness is an act of trust and obedience in your good Father. Forgiveness is the way to joy!

Think About It

Who do you need to forgive? Make a list of the people who have hurt or offended you.

_____

_____

_____

_____

_____

_____

_____

_____

_____

_____

_____

_____

_____

_____

_____

_____

_____

_____

_____

_____

_____

_____

_____

_____

_____

_____

_____

If you have forgiven them, write about that experience.

_____

_____

_____

_____

_____

_____

_____

_____

_____

_____

_____

_____

_____

_____

_____

_____

_____

_____

_____

_____

_____

_____

_____

_____

_____

_____

_____

_____

_____

How has forgiveness changed you or set you free?

Have you been confused about what it means to forgive?

_____

_____

_____

_____

_____

_____

_____

_____

_____

_____

_____

_____

_____

_____

_____

_____

_____

_____

_____

_____

_____

_____

_____

_____

_____

_____

_____

_____

_____

If you know you still need to forgive someone, write about how unforgiveness has kept you locked up in a prison. Why is it hard to forgive that person?

_____

_____

_____

_____

_____

_____

_____

_____

_____

_____

_____

_____

_____

_____

_____

_____

_____

_____

_____

_____

_____

_____

_____

_____

_____

Write Your Story

Now, write your story on _Forgiveness_ that you will share with your group:

_____

_____

_____

_____

_____

_____

_____

_____

_____

_____

_____

_____

_____

_____

_____

_____

_____

_____

_____

_____

_____

_____

_____

_____

_____

_____

_____

_____

_____

Listen for the Sound of Heaven

After you have shared your story in your group write what the Lord spoke to you through your friends. What did He say? What is stirring in your heart?

_____

_____

_____

_____

_____

_____

_____

_____

_____

_____

_____

_____

_____

_____

_____

_____

_____

_____

_____

_____

_____

_____

_____

_____

_____

_____

_____

_____

Rewrite the Story

Do you need to do any REWRITING in your story? If so, write about the lie you were believing regarding forgiveness and rewrite the story in truth.

_____

_____

_____

_____

_____

_____

_____

_____

_____

_____

_____

_____

_____

_____

_____

_____

_____

_____

_____

_____

_____

_____

_____

_____

_____

_____

_____

_____

Story 9

Moving Past Fear

Fear can be crippling, irrational and insane, and ruin your life. Fear can also be the very thing that unleashes your greatest potential. Moving past your fear can usher in the freedom to be who God has called you to be!

Fear resists faith.

Our best life requires faith. Real life is hard. There is pain and heartbreak all around you. People are dying–in every sense of the word. You are needed. Your beauty is needed. Your gifts are needed. What stops you from entering into the battle of loving people well, living vulnerable, staying compassionate, and daring to be courageously, imperfectly YOU?

Fear.

What are you afraid of?

God sees you, longing and hurting. He comes to you in this messy, broken place. His nail scarred hands open. He asks you to give Him your pain, hurt, and disappointment. In return He will give you a mission, a vision, a passion that has long since been buried or denied. Do you know this passion that makes your soul come alive?

And what if your pain, covered in fear, was the only way to unmask that dream deep within you?

You have a call on your life and a destiny only you can fulfill. Fear will be the enemy you need to name, and defeat, in order to walk into your destiny.

"For God has not given us a spirit of fear and timidity, but of power, love, and self-discipline."
2 Timothy 1:7 NLT

Think About It

What are you afraid of? What is the fear that keeps you small, afraid, ashamed?

_____

_____

_____

_____

_____

_____

_____

_____

_____

_____

_____

_____

_____

_____

_____

_____

_____

_____

_____

_____

_____

_____

_____

_____

_____

_____

What were you doing when you felt your soul come to life? (Hint: You might have been acting fearlessly!) What hobbies, talents, activities, etc. bring you great joy?

Did you know the opposite of fear is love? What words of love has the Father whispered into your fear?

_____

_____

_____

_____

_____

_____

_____

_____

_____

_____

_____

_____

_____

_____

_____

_____

_____

_____

_____

_____

_____

_____

_____

_____

_____

_____

_____

_____

_____

_____

Is fear still at work? Did you know that fear would keep you from your purpose? Then ask God what words of love will break those chains of fear.

_____

_____

_____

_____

_____

_____

_____

_____

_____

_____

_____

_____

_____

_____

_____

_____

_____

_____

_____

_____

_____

_____

_____

_____

_____

_____

_____

_____

<u>Write Your Story</u>

Now, write your story on *<u>Moving Past Fear</u>* that you will share with your group:

_____

_____

_____

_____

_____

_____

_____

_____

_____

_____

_____

_____

_____

_____

_____

_____

_____

_____

_____

_____

_____

_____

_____

_____

_____

_____

_____

_____

_____

_____

Listen for the Sound of Heaven

After you have shared your story write what the Lord spoke to you through your friends. What did He say? What is stirring in your heart?

_____

_____

_____

_____

_____

_____

_____

_____

_____

_____

_____

_____

_____

_____

_____

_____

_____

_____

_____

_____

_____

_____

_____

_____

_____

Rewrite the Story

Do you need to do any REWRITING in your story? If so, write about the lie you were believing regarding fear and rewrite the story in truth.

_____

_____

_____

_____

_____

_____

_____

_____

_____

_____

_____

_____

_____

_____

_____

_____

_____

_____

_____

_____

_____

_____

_____

_____

_____

_____

_____

_____

_____

_____
_____
_____
_____
_____
_____
_____
_____
_____
_____
_____
_____
_____
_____
_____
_____
_____
_____
_____
_____
_____
_____
_____
_____
_____
_____
_____
_____
_____
_____
_____
_____

Story 10

Navigating Relationships

Relationships are, without a doubt, the richest gift of God. In them we find love, belonging, comfort, joy, acceptance, and significance. Unless we don't. This very hard reality can create a significant amount of hurt in our lives.

From the beginning we were created to be in community, fashioned for intimacy, unity, and belonging. This perfect unity and intimacy is meant to be found in God first. He is your First Love. All the other people are meant to be blessings. We often look to human relationships and wonder why they don't really satisfy us. We wonder why we feel disappointed, disconnected, alone, unloved, and unknown by the people in our life. Typically, our response is to blame the other person, leave them, shut down, or ignore the hunger inside our souls for more authentic connection.

But true intimacy is experienced by placing people behind God, not above God. You must look to God for the fulfillment of your deepest needs. Then, and only then, can you enjoy the beautiful gift of healthy relationships.

The first step is always personal responsibility. Own your stuff. Look at your motives. Determine if you are loving others "to get something" from them. Becoming your true self requires you change the way you have related in unhealthy ways towards the people in your life.

Relationships are work. They require selfless acts, generous amounts of grace and forgiveness, acceptance, and vulnerability.

When operating in Christ's design the end result is fulfillment and joy.

"We love because He first loved us."
1 John 4:19 ESV

Think About It

Write about a hard relationship.

_____

_____

_____

_____

_____

_____

_____

_____

_____

_____

_____

_____

_____

_____

_____

_____

_____

_____

_____

_____

_____

_____

_____

_____

_____

_____

_____

_____

_____

_____

_____

What are you longing for in that relationship? What are you looking for?

_____

_____

_____

_____

_____

_____

_____

_____

_____

_____

_____

_____

_____

_____

_____

_____

_____

_____

_____

_____

_____

_____

_____

_____

_____

_____

_____

What is God speaking to you about loving this person above yourself?

_____

_____

_____

_____

_____

_____

_____

_____

_____

_____

_____

_____

_____

_____

_____

_____

_____

_____

_____

_____

_____

_____

_____

_____

_____

_____

_____

_____

_____

_____

_____

What are the changes you can make to walk in His love in this relationship? Ask God for clarity and wisdom as you seek to hear his heart.

_____

_____

_____

_____

_____

_____

_____

_____

_____

_____

_____

_____

_____

_____

_____

_____

_____

_____

_____

_____

_____

_____

_____

_____

_____

_____

_____

_____

_____

_____

_____

_____

_____

Write about a deep friendship. What did it take to build this friendship? What makes it such a gift?

Write Your Story

Now, write your story on <u>*Navigating Relationships*</u> that you will share with your group:

_____

_____

_____

_____

_____

_____

_____

_____

_____

_____

_____

_____

_____

_____

_____

_____

_____

_____

_____

_____

_____

_____

_____

_____

_____

_____

_____

Listen for the Sound of Heaven

After you have shared your story write what the Lord spoke to you through your friends. What did He say? What is stirring in your heart?

_____

_____

_____

_____

_____

_____

_____

_____

_____

_____

_____

_____

_____

_____

_____

_____

_____

_____

_____

_____

_____

_____

_____

_____

_____

_____

_____

_____

_____

_____

_____

_____

_____

_____

_____

_____

_____

_____

_____

_____

_____

_____

_____

_____

_____

_____

_____

_____

_____

_____

_____

_____

_____

Rewrite the Story

Do you need to do any REWRITING in your story? If so, write about the lie you were believing regarding relationships and rewrite the story in truth.

_____

_____

_____

_____

_____

_____

_____

_____

_____

_____

_____

_____

_____

_____

_____

_____

_____

_____

_____

_____

_____

_____

_____

_____

_____

_____

_____

_____

Story 11

Real Transformation

We constantly indulge in the drink of toxic thinking. Taking big gulps and ingesting the lies, we wonder why our lives are in chaos. We wonder why there are those nagging "issues" and broken relationships. We wonder why we do the very things we hate.

Justifying our minor struggles against the bigger sins of life we tend to look at our small infractions as lesser evils–shopping and spending over our budget, yelling at the kids, eating too much, drinking a bit more often than usual–but we feel it in our souls. There is an emptiness that invades, a sense of futility and frustration, with people and life in general. It is easier to blame and judge others, than deal with the "why" behind our feelings of dissatisfaction, hopelessness, and anger.

But we will always behave according to what we believe.

Underneath it all there is a starting point. Triggers from past events or people's choices send messages to our brains that carry hard feelings we want to avoid. We cannot help but react to the fear and trauma of the past **IF** we have not named the poison that came with it. The poison, the lies and whispers of the enemy, can only be destroyed by our Father's good and perfect words over our life.

God calls you to stop this pattern and renew your mind to a new thought process. Determine to operate in the Spirit of God within you and take responsibility for the words you let into your soul! The choice will always be yours.

"I have set before you life and death, now choose life."
Deuteronomy 30:19 NIV

*"We demolish arguments and every pretension that sets itself
up against the knowledge of God, and we take captive every
thought and make it obedient to Christ."*
2 Corinthians 10:5 NIV

This is God's design for your soul! You're meant to think the truth
and operate in love! It's in this beautiful process that God will do
the work to infuse in you His God-given truths of Heaven! You
can't create this new life. God will do the work. You must learn
to get still. Engage in the process of identifying what the real
battle is – the faulty thinking that led you to the toxic behavior.
Sit with it. Invite God in. Ask Him to give you a new way to live.
A way that takes every thought and replaces it with truth! A way
which will lead you to your transformed life!

Think About It

Think about a current struggle and get to the heart of the matter.

Write about the event. Then name the negative thought, the feeling it evokes, the flood of more negative thoughts, then the sin (your behaviors, your false self) you engage in. See it as a cycle.

_____

_____

_____

_____

_____

_____

_____

_____

_____

_____

_____

_____

_____

_____

_____

_____

_____

_____

_____

_____

_____

_____

_____

_____

Where did the toxic thought begin? Have you struggled with this thought before?

_____

_____

_____

_____

_____

_____

_____

_____

_____

_____

_____

_____

_____

_____

_____

_____

_____

_____

_____

_____

_____

_____

_____

_____

_____

_____

_____

_____

_____

What is the truth that God is calling you to believe? This is your true self as a beloved child of God! (You may need the help of your friends here if you cannot name the truth. Be brave and ask.)

_____

_____

_____

_____

_____

_____

_____

_____

_____

_____

_____

_____

_____

_____

_____

_____

_____

_____

_____

_____

_____

_____

_____

_____

_____

Now, envision yourself believing the truth. What feelings does the truth evoke? What other thoughts (truths) flood your mind? What different behaviors do you imagine you will engage in now?

_____

_____

_____

_____

_____

_____

_____

_____

_____

_____

_____

_____

_____

_____

_____

_____

_____

_____

_____

_____

_____

_____

_____

_____

_____

_____

_____

Write Your Story

Now, write your story on <u>*Real Transformation: A Lie Renamed in Truth*</u> that you will share with your group:

_____

_____

_____

_____

_____

_____

_____

_____

_____

_____

_____

_____

_____

_____

_____

_____

_____

_____

_____

_____

_____

_____

_____

_____

_____

_____

_____
_____
_____
_____
_____
_____
_____
_____
_____
_____
_____
_____
_____
_____
_____
_____
_____
_____
_____
_____
_____
_____
_____
_____
_____
_____
_____
_____
_____
_____

Listen for the Sound of Heaven

After you have shared your story write what the Lord spoke to you through your friends. What did He say? What is stirring in your heart?

_____

_____

_____

_____

_____

_____

_____

_____

_____

_____

_____

_____

_____

_____

_____

_____

_____

_____

_____

_____

_____

_____

_____

_____

Rewrite the Story

Do you need to do any REWRITING in your story? If so, write about the lie you were believing from the enemy and rewrite the story in truth.

_____

_____

_____

_____

_____

_____

_____

_____

_____

_____

_____

_____

_____

_____

_____

_____

_____

_____

_____

_____

_____

_____

_____

_____

Story 12

A Surrendered Heart

The great struggle of life is to get over ourselves. Get over our feelings, our wants, our needs. We are a self-centered people.

But this is not your true self. You were made to love well, embrace suffering, and give your life away. You were made to give lavishly and generously to those in need, to sow seeds of kindness, mercy, and grace. You were made for so much more than this world. You were never meant to find your home here. You were born to die - to your natural self. You were made to bring Heaven to Earth by the way you willingly lay down your self-centered ways and operate in the love, kindness, and goodness of God.

> *"If you cling to your life, you will lose it; but if you give it up*
> *your life for me, you will find it."*
> Matthew 10:39 NLT

> *"This then is how you should pray, 'Our Father in Heaven,*
> *hallowed by your name, your kingdom come, your will be done,*
> *on earth as it is in Heaven'."*
> Matthew 6:9,10 NIV

This beautiful journey of trusting God, living with vulnerability, courage, and grace will mean nothing if you choose to hold on to the very things God is asking you to let go of. Grasping for life, holding on to the things of this world, in hopes of finding satisfaction and fulfillment, will never be enough. This life is but a quick breath. Often we live as if this life is all there is. There is so much more.

Destiny is not always found in the things that have brought happiness. Sometimes, our destiny is birthed through a loss or a death. Trusting God in the middle of the grief takes faith that the goodness of God, his character, and your identity are unshakable through it all.

Your real life will be found in the hard places–the times of suffering, surrender, and pain. It is here God will comfort you, so you can comfort others. It is here God will whisper the truths of Heaven to your soul, so you can bring the very sound of Heaven to Earth! Will you let go now? Will you let go of the things that are holding you captive to a world that is not your home? Will you whisper to your good Father, your faithful Friend, your Creator, and Beloved…

Not my will, but yours be done.
Luke 22:42 NIV

Let Heaven come!

Think About It

What things of this world are you grasping on to, afraid to let go?

_____

_____

_____

_____

_____

_____

_____

_____

_____

_____

_____

_____

_____

_____

_____

_____

_____

_____

_____

_____

_____

_____

_____

_____

_____

Where is God speaking to you, ushering you into a kind of death, so you might find your life?

_____

_____

_____

_____

_____

_____

_____

_____

_____

_____

_____

_____

_____

_____

_____

_____

_____

_____

_____

_____

_____

_____

_____

_____

_____

___ _____

___ _____

_____

_____

_____

What would it look like to bring Heaven to Earth? What does it mean to believe you were made to reflect the image of God to those around you?

_____

_____

_____

_____

_____

_____

_____

_____

_____

_____

_____

_____

_____

_____

_____

_____

_____

_____

_____

_____

_____

_____

_____

_____

Write Your Story

Now, write your story on _A Surrender Heart_ that you will share with your group:

_____

_____

_____

_____

_____

_____

_____

_____

_____

_____

_____

_____

_____

_____

_____

_____

_____

_____

_____

_____

_____

_____

_____

_____

_____

_____

_____

_____

Listen for the Sound of Heaven

After you have shared your story write what the Lord spoke to you through your friends. What did He say? What is stirring in your heart?

_____

_____

_____

_____

_____

_____

_____

_____

_____

_____

_____

_____

_____

_____

_____

_____

_____

_____

_____

_____

_____

_____

_____

_____

Rewrite the Story

Do you need to do any REWRITING in your story? If so, write about the lie you were believing regarding surrender and rewrite the story in truth.

_____

_____

_____

_____

_____

_____

_____

_____

_____

_____

_____

_____

_____

_____

_____

_____

_____

_____

_____

_____

_____

_____

_____

_____

_____

Afterword

You did it!

I'm so proud of you and your friends! I would love to get a glimpse into your story and hear how God is setting your soul free to live a wholehearted life through the power of authentic, truth-filled community! You can share stories and experiences by emailing me at nicoleedgmond@gmail.com or share a story on your social media pages with the hashtag #bravingthebrokenness.

I would love for you to join me and some beautiful friends for an evening of feasting on food, fellowship, and truth! Life is better together. *GATHER* is a quarterly Story Night that is hosted locally. Check my Instagram page @nicoleedgmond for dates, location, and details for our next gathering! I would love to meet you! #gather #togetherintruth

If you have found healing and growth through this process, would you consider leading another group of friends? This is the power of our freedom. We were made to help others set their soul free! It is my desire to see every story redeemed, and every daughter or son walking in their God-given destiny!

Keep on writing! The best is yet to come!

CPSIA information can be obtained
at www.ICGtesting.com
Printed in the USA
LVHW051108210521
688045LV00012B/830

9 781545 679111